Life in the Old West

Who Settled the West?

Bobbie Kalman

🌱 Crabtree Publishing Company

www.crabtreebooks.com

LIFE IN THE OLD WEST

Created by Bobbie Kalman

To my grandparents, George and June Little, who settled the West

Author and Editor-in-Chief
Bobbie Kalman

Managing editor
Lynda Hale

Senior editor
April Fast

Project editor
John Crossingham

Researcher
Sarah Dann

Copy editors
Kate Calder
Heather Levigne

Photo research
John Crossingham

Special thanks to
Pecos National Historical Park; LaVaughn
Breshanan, Wyoming State Archives; Nancy
Sherbert, Kansas State Historical Society;
Thora Cooke, Western Canada Pictorial Index;
Confederation Life Group of Companies;
Glenbow Archives

Computer design
Lynda Hale
Rob MacGregor (cover concept)
Campbell Creative Services

Production coordinator
Hannelore Sotzek

Crabtree Publishing Company

www.crabtreebooks.com   1-800-387-7650

Copyright © **1999 CRABTREE PUBLISHING COMPANY**.
All rights reserved. No part of this publication may be reproduced,
stored in a retrieval system or be transmitted in any form or by
any means, electronic, mechanical, photocopying, recording, or
otherwise, without the prior written permission of Crabtree
Publishing Company. In Canada: We acknowledge the financial
support of the Government of Canada through the Canada Book
Fund for our publishing activities.

Printed in Canada/042013/MA20130325

Library of Congress Cataloging in Publication Data
Kalman, Bobbie
   Who settled the West?

(Life in the Old West)
Includes index.
ISBN 0-7787-0075-5 (library bound) ISBN 0-7787-0107-7 (pbk.)
This book discusses the reasons people migrated West, the routes
they took, the difficulties they faced, the different ethnic and cultural backgrounds of the settlers,
and the building of homes and towns.
1. Pioneers—West (North America)—History—Juvenile literature. 2. Frontier and pioneer life—
West (North America)—Juvenile literature. 3. Migration, Internal—North America—History—
Juvenile literature. 4. West (North America)—History—Juvenile literature. [1. Pioneers—West
(North America). 2. Frontier and pioneer life—West (North America). 3. West (North America)—
History.] I. Title. II. Series: Kalman, Bobbie. Life in the Old West.
F591.K18 1999   j978   LC 99-11528
                                                                                  CIP

Published in Canada
Crabtree Publishing
616 Welland Ave.
St. Catharines, Ontario
L2M 5V6

Published in the United States
Crabtree Publishing
PMB 59051
350 Fifth Avenue, 59th Floor
New York, New York 10118

Published in the United Kingdom
Crabtree Publishing
Maritime House
Basin Road North, Hove
BN41 1WR

Published in Australia
Crabtree Publishing
3 Charles Street
Coburg North
VIC, 3058

TABLE OF CONTENTS

France occupied what is now eastern Canada and the central United States. Britain's colonies were located in the eastern United States and Canada, and Spain claimed Florida, Mexico, and areas in the southwestern United States. Russia owned Alaska until 1867.

In the 1600s, the United States, Canada, and Mexico were not yet countries. Instead, North America was made up of several **colonies**. A colony is a territory that is ruled by another country. The colonies belonged to England, Spain, and France. The western part of North America, however, was unexplored by the Europeans. In the mid-1800s, settlers began migrating to this area of land.

The Great Plains

The landscape of the West varied greatly. In the center of North America lay a large area of flat, grassy land called the Great Plains. A person could look for miles in every direction and see nothing but flat, open land. Native Americans lived there and hunted the buffalo herds that roamed freely. Thousands of settlers made the Great Plains their new home.

The Southwest

The Southwest had large desert areas where few plants and animals lived. Other areas in the Southwest, however, had rivers and fertile farmland. Cattle ranches were popular in these areas, which provided grasses for grazing.

The Rockies

The Rocky Mountains divided the Great Plains and the west coast. The uneven slopes and sudden snowstorms in the Rockies claimed the lives of many settlers. Many crossed the Rockies successfully, however, and settled in areas that are now Oregon, California, and British Columbia.

The west coast

On the west side of the Rocky Mountains, the land was green and lush. The soil in the rolling hills and valleys was ideal for growing crops and fruit trees. Giant trees called redwoods grew in the forests.

THE FIRST PEOPLES

The Native Americans were the first inhabitants of the West. They lived there thousands of years before the Europeans arrived. The lifestyle of the Native Americans differed, depending on where they lived and to which nation they belonged. On the Great Plains, **nomadic**, or wandering, nations such as the Sioux followed and hunted buffalo for food and clothing. They lived in tents called **tipis**.

The Haida and Tlingit of the Northwest built permanent wooden homes called **longhouses**. The people of these nations made large canoes and giant **totem poles** out of tree trunks. The southwestern nations, such as the Navajo and Pecos, were farmers who built clay homes called **pueblos**. A pueblo, shown below, had many levels. The people who lived in these buildings were also known as the Pueblo.

Respect for the land

Native Americans believed that they were part of nature. The natural world gave them everything they needed—food, shelter, water, and clothing. Native Americans respected the land, animals, plants, and water and believed that these natural resources belonged to all living things. They took from nature only what they needed in order to survive. Many European settlers, however, took more than they needed and soon used up much of the natural resources.

European conquest

The Europeans had beliefs that were different from those of the Native Americans. They wanted to build their homes on the unsettled land. They did not care that they were changing the Native way of life. The settlers claimed more and more land until the Native Nations were pushed out of most of their homelands. The settlers killed millions of buffalo, often just for sport, leaving many Native Nations without food. European armies and diseases also killed thousands of Native Americans.

The first Europeans to settle in the West were the Spaniards. Their colony, which started in the 1500s, was called New Spain. It covered territories that are now Texas, Mexico, New Mexico, Arizona, California, and Florida. For many years, the Spaniards were very powerful, and New Spain was the largest colony in North America.

Spanish missions

Spain was a Roman Catholic country. Roman Catholics are Christians who belong to the Roman Catholic Church. Spanish priests called **missionaries** came to New Spain to **convert**, or change the religious beliefs of, the Native Americans. They set up villages called **missions**. The mission buildings were made of the same materials as pueblos. Native Americans who converted were called **neophytes**.

Life at the mission

Neophytes learned to speak Spanish and dressed in European clothing. They prayed many times during the day. Many neophytes grew tired of their new life, but the missionaries were reluctant to let them leave. They were afraid the neophytes would forget about Christianity if they left the mission. The missionaries also depended on the neophytes to farm the land and work around the mission.

Birth of the ranch

The Spaniards also set up **ranches** where they raised the horses and cattle they brought with them from Spain. They used the cattle's hide to make leather. The **tallow**, or fat of cattle, was used to make candles and soap. The Spaniards taught the Native Americans how to ride horses, herd cattle, and hunt with guns.

The fur traders

Many Europeans who lived in the West were involved in the fur trade. These trappers and hunters, known as **mountain men**, traveled into the mountains in search of wild animals. By the time the settlers arrived, few bears, cougars, and other large animals were left. Some mountain men made a living guiding settlers to their new homesteads.

Hudson's Bay Company

The Hudson's Bay Company was a fur-trading business in North America. It was founded by the British government, who owned most of the territories in Canada. The company had **trading posts** all across northern North America. At these posts, trappers and hunters traded beaver, deer, bear, wolf, and other furs for food and supplies. When the early settlers came to the West, some of them also got involved with the fur trade.

(above) The mountain men transported their furs to trading posts by canoe. (below) Fort Edmonton in Canada was an early western fur-trading settlement.

The Louisiana Purchase (1803)

(above) After the United States purchased Louisiana, the country was nearly as large as New Spain. During the 1800s, America claimed the northern section of New Spain, as well as the southern half of Oregon Territory.

By the 1800s, the European colonies were becoming independent. In 1776, the United States became a country. Colonists in New Spain formed Mexico in 1821. Canada's colonies united in 1867.

What a deal!

During the early 1800s, the French were busy fighting wars in Europe. France did not have enough soldiers to protect its colony. The country also needed money. France's land in North America, which was called the Louisiana Territory, included the Mississippi River. This river was a popular transportation route. In 1803, American ambassadors went to France to buy a couple of French-owned sea ports in North America. Instead, they bought the entire Louisiana Territory from France for $15 million! This doubled America's size overnight.

The new western ranches

When people in the East heard about the new land, they headed west. There were also free cattle available. The cattle that the Spaniards had brought to North America hundreds of years ago had multiplied and were roaming wild. Many people set up cattle ranches and sold the cattle for their beef. The American ranchers learned how to raise cattle from the *vaqueros*. *Vaqueros* were Mexican cowboys who lived in areas that were once part of New Spain. Many *vaqueros* worked at the new ranches.

The race west

People in the United States and Canada became more interested in the West. They heard stories about rich ranchers, huge areas of unused land, and gold finds. The two countries grew fearful that they might lose this land to each other or Mexico. They needed citizens to go and occupy the land in order to keep it. Both governments offered cheap land to anyone who claimed it, and the race to settle the West began!

*(above) The western gold rushes attracted thousands of people. **Prospectors** searched for gold alone or in groups. Although most prospectors expected to return home after they found gold, many settled in the West.*

(opposite page bottom) Ranches were popular in the West.

The Mormon migration

The Mormons are a religious group who lived in Illinois in the early 1800s. Their religion was not liked by others, and they were often attacked for their beliefs. In 1847, their leader, Brigham Young, decided the Mormons should move 1300 miles (2092 kilometers) west to Salt Lake Valley, an isolated place where they hoped to practice their religion in peace. Young left with 144 Mormons in search of the valley. Some pulled heavy carts by hand because they could not afford mules, oxen, or covered wagons. Eventually, over 3000 Mormons arrived in what is now Utah and began building a city. Despite having poor farmland, Salt Lake City became a thriving Mormon community.

Between the 1600s and 1865, many African Americans were **slaves** on **plantations** in the southern United States. Plantations were large farms that grew one type of crop such as cotton or tobacco. Americans sailed to Africa and captured people to be their slaves. Many Africans were separated from their families when they were brought to North America. Slaves were forced to work long hours without pay and were kept against their will. They were beaten if they disobeyed orders.

Escaping slavery

Slavery was not legal everywhere in North America. Canada and most of the northern states of America did not practice slavery. Many slaves risked their life attempting to escape to the North. If an owner caught a slave who had tried to escape, he beat the slave severely. Many slaves were killed by their owners after trying to run to freedom.

Heading west

Besides the North, another place that offered safety to slaves was the West. Slavery was not legal in the West, and African Americans could find paid work there. Some escaped to ranches and became cowboys. After slavery became illegal, African Americans left the southern states in large numbers. Many started their own businesses in western towns. Others bought land and set up farms. Many African American families lived peacefully in the West.

Moving to Canada

Hundreds of slaves had escaped to Canada during the years of slavery in the southern states. Canada provided opportunities for many African Americans. Some made a new life for themselves as farmers and businessmen in the Canadian West. They brought with them the skills they had learned as slaves on the southern plantations.

*Southern plantations were terrible places for African Americans to live. The **Thirteenth Amendment**, passed by the United States government in 1865, made slavery illegal and allowed African Americans to migrate to the West.*

Even though they were free, African Americans often encountered hostility from their neighbors. **Prejudice** *did not stop them from moving to the West, however, where many prospered. This African American family built a sod house on the prairie. Some members of the family worked as slaves before slavery became illegal.*

This man is a cook on a western cattle drive. Many African Americans found work as cowboys.

John Ware was a well-known Canadian cowboy. He owned a cattle ranch near Red Deer River.

TRAVELING OVER LAND

A well-organized wagon train could travel up to 20 miles (32 kilometers) a day. Wagon trains that ran into bad weather or difficult terrain sometimes took a couple of weeks to travel 50 miles (80 kilometers).

The early settlers of the West traveled in covered wagons pulled by mules or oxen. As many as 200 wagons formed a **wagon train**, although some trains were smaller. Wagon trains followed rough trails beaten into the ground by wagons that had traveled before them. The trip from east to west took several months and was very difficult.

A long, harsh journey

Conditions on the wagon trains were harsh, and settlers were exposed to extreme weather. Heavy rains flooded rivers, making them impossible to cross, and turned trails into thick mud. Food and water often ran out, and many people starved or became dehydrated in the intense heat. Travelers were exhausted by the long days and difficult conditions. People became so weak that diseases spread quickly. Without doctors, settlers found it difficult to help the sick, and many people died.

Take the train

Travel improved dramatically with the completion of cross-country railway lines. By the late 1800s, both the United States and Canada had long lines of track stretching into the West. First-class cars were like expensive hotels on wheels. Even third-class passengers traveled in comfort compared to a wagon-train journey. The western railroads cost a lot of money to build, but they quickly proved their worth. They carried thousands of settlers to their new homes and helped populate the West.

After hearing many horror stories about traveling by wagon train, everyone was eager to take the train!
*The **transcontinental lines** completed in the United States and Canada were a great source of pride.*

Many Americans moved from the East to the West, but they were not the only settlers. Hundreds of thousands of **immigrants** from Europe and Asia also came to settle in the West. An immigrant is a person who leaves his or her country to live in another country. Immigrants crossed oceans to begin new lives.

A different world

Many immigrants came from countries that were very different from North America. European and Asian cities had been around for hundreds of years. Places such as China, Prussia, and Austria-Hungary were home to huge, crowded populations. There were not enough jobs or money for everyone, and there were constant wars among the countries. Some people were not allowed to practice their religion, and many were unable to own land or a home.

Spreading the news

The government of both the United States and Canada wanted its country to stretch from ocean to ocean. Both countries needed to bring people to the West to increase the population. They spent large amounts of money advertising land in the West to people in Europe. Millions of advertisements were distributed in different languages all over Europe. They promoted the West as the best place to live and repeatedly mentioned the low cost of farmland.

Land of opportunity

Businesses such as railroad companies also helped promote the West by offering people jobs. Agents were sent overseas to let people know about the many opportunities in the West. The agents set up displays at county fairs and had offices in major shipping ports. They encouraged people to move to the West and offered to help immigrants with moving arrangements. The government even paid hundreds of western settlers to go back to their European homelands and spread the word about moving to the West.

People around the world began to see the West as the answer to all their problems. It offered cheap land, religious freedom, no taxes, and plenty of jobs. People were willing to leave their home and family behind to go after their dreams in North America.

Difficult journey

Those who decided to move west had a tough journey ahead of them. Most settlers had little money and could not afford to travel in comfort. Communicating with officials, agents, and other passengers was difficult because everyone spoke different languages.

Sickness at sea

Some immigrants traveled hundreds of miles to board ships that took them across the ocean to North America. This ocean voyage took seven days in good weather but could be three weeks long if there were storms. Many passengers became violently seasick and dehydrated.

The ships were crowded, and dangerous diseases spread among the passengers. The passengers with the least money were kept in the ship's **hold**, or bottom. If the weather was stormy, the hold was sealed, and people were not allowed in or out, even if they were sick or hungry.

(opposite page) Although it was sad to say goodbye to family and friends, these immigrants set sail for North America with high hopes and big dreams!

When the immigrants arrived in North America, they were given a checkup. If a doctor decided that someone was unhealthy, he or she was sent back home. Sometimes sick children were separated from their family because the parents could not afford to buy a ticket to go home with their child.

What was your name again?

Many settlers arrived from Austria-Hungary. Austria-Hungary had taken over most of the countries in Eastern Europe. Austrians, Hungarians, Slavs, and Ukrainians were all Austro-Hungarians. Immigration officers found it difficult to classify settlers from these countries. They often guessed incorrectly the homelands of the immigrants or spelled their names wrong. The immigrants could not speak English to correct the error, so their names were changed forever.

Austro-Hungarians settled all over the West, especially on the plains, where the land was similar to that of Europe. This Slavic family is putting the finishing touches on their new home. They are spreading a mud paste over the walls to seal the holes between the logs. The mud kept out much of the wind during the cold winter.

YOUR ALLIES THE JUGO-SLAVS

Each culture within Austria-Hungary had its own religion, language, and lifestyle. Immigrants from Romania, Hungary, Poland, and the Ukraine left their homeland to escape the terrible conditions of war, starvation, and unemployment. These Yugoslav immigrants gather for a photograph in their new country. Many are wearing the traditional clothing of their homeland.

(above) In Scotland, farms were called **crofts**. Many Scottish farmers, called **crofters**, left their homeland to start farms in the West. Scotland's climate and land were similar to the northern areas of the West, and the crofters prospered on their new land.

(below) Many Irish settlers worked in the construction of western canals, roadways, and railroads. Once this work was finished, the Irish workers became residents in many of the towns built along these transportation lines.

Scandinavia is made up of the countries of Sweden, Norway, Finland, and Denmark. Millions of Scandinavians left their homelands to live in western North America for different reasons. People from Denmark left because of problems in their church. Finns were ruled unfairly by the Russian government. Swedes experienced severe crop failures and low-paying jobs. Many Scandinavians settled in the northern plains of the United States and Canada because the weather was similar to that of their homeland.

Icelanders left their homes to escape a food shortage. Many settled in Gimli, Manitoba. This Canadian town's name meant "paradise." It was not quite heaven for the first few years, however. Diseases such as smallpox killed a quarter of the Icelandic population. Despite this tragedy, the Icelanders stayed and established a strong farming community.

Many Italians worked on the railroad or in the mines. Their jobs were organized by a sponsor called a *patrone*. A *patrone* helped Italian immigrants find work. The first Italians in the West often went home to their families during the winter when their work term was over. As the towns became more developed, however, they brought their families to live in the West and made it their permanent home.

Religious groups such as Jews, Mennonites, Hutterites, and Dukhobors lived throughout Europe and Asia. When they came west, they all wanted religious freedom. At home, they were rarely allowed to worship in peace. The United States and Canada offered religious freedom and cheap land—two very good reasons for immigration. Many Jewish families started businesses in towns. The Mennonites (top and center) often lived together in large houses. Hutterites (bottom left and right) and Dukhobors worked hard to establish farms on the prairies.

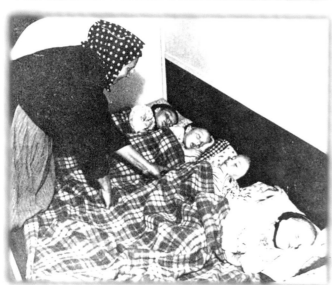

(above left and right) Thousands of Chinese men came to the West to work in the mines and help build the railroad. They did the most dangerous jobs, lived under poor conditions, and were paid low wages. The Chinese had a very different culture from that of North Americans and Europeans and were often treated with hostility. Although most Chinese came to earn money for their families in China, many later brought their families to settle in the West.

Most Japanese settlers did not begin arriving until the early 1900s. By this time, many western towns were built and well-established. Most Japanese immigrants settled in these towns and started restaurants and other service businesses.

When settlers arrived at their new land, they had to **stake their claim**, or determine which land was theirs. Newcomers had to settle land-claim problems themselves. Later on, the government set up land-claim offices to handle the growing number of immigrants. At these offices, officials had maps that showed which land was still available. Settlers went there to choose their homestead.

Getting ready for the first winter

After their land claim was secure, the newcomers prepared the land for farming. It did not take long for winter snows to blanket the land. The settlers set up tents or built crude shelters out of materials they found.

Clearing the land of trees and boulders was tiring. These settlers worked hard to build their new home!

The first homes

On the plains, the simplest home built by settlers was the **dugout**. A dugout was a large hole in the side of a small hill with a wall and roof added to it. **Sod**, or soil, bricks were used to build houses called **soddies**. **Log homes** were made by stacking long logs with notches cut into the ends. **Frame houses** were built in places with sawmills. Wood was cut into thin planks and nailed to a wooden frame.

Clearing the woods

Settlers who lived in the forests had to clear their land before it could be farmed. Unlike the flat plains, forests had thousands of trees and large rocks. Settlers cut down tree after tree. They then used oxen or horses to pull stubborn tree stumps and boulders out of the ground.

Warmth and food

The fireplace provided heat for warmth and cooking, as well as light. Keeping the fire burning was extremely important, especially in winter. If settlers did not have wood for their fires, they used **cow chips**, or dried cow manure. To provide their family with food, the settlers hunted animals and began growing crops as soon as they could. They gathered food in the autumn and stored it for use in winter.

Health problems

Settlers who fell ill often used home remedies to treat their sickness. Home remedies rarely cured serious diseases, however, and these diseases often spread to other members of the family. There were few doctors in the West, and many people died without proper medical attention.

These settlers were proud of their soddy. The thick walls protected them from harsh winter winds and hot summer sun.

FIELDS OF DREAMS

Most settlers were farmers. The West had a huge amount of land available, but farming it was not easy. Settlers worked hard to harvest their fields. They did most of the work by hand, and the whole family helped. They made their clothing and tools from whatever they could find, raise, or grow.

Useful animals

Animals were important to the settlers. They provided food and clothing. Cows gave milk, and chickens laid eggs. Settlers also kept these animals for their meat. Sheep's wool was needed for warm clothing in the harsh winters. Oxen and horses pulled wagons and plows and hauled wood and supplies to and from the local town. Plowing was a difficult task, especially on new land. The plow often got caught on roots and rocks in the thick, hard soil.

Growing crops

Corn was the most popular crop in the West. Farmers grew it in great quantities. The settlers started growing other things as well. Rye, barley, and wheat were all common crops. A good harvest was necessary for a family's survival. It not only gave the settlers food, it also fed the livestock. The family exchanged extra crops for other goods or earned money by selling their crops to buyers in the cities. The crops were then transported across the continent by railroad.

Frost and fires

A successful year on a western farm was partly due to luck. Farmers who planted their seeds too early often lost them to a late frost which killed the seeds. Grass fires sometimes swept across the prairie, burning crops and homes in their path.

Droughts and locusts

Farmers also lived in constant fear of long periods without rain called **droughts**. During a drought, nothing could grow. **Locusts** were another threat. Locusts are grasshoppers that travel in huge groups. In some years, swarms of locusts ate entire fields of farmers' crops.

Using their special farming skills

Many immigrants tried to settle in areas where the land was similar to that of their homeland. Mennonites were skilled at farming the open land of Russia and the Ukraine. They used their skills to farm the land of the prairies that was far away from rivers and lakes. Many Italians looked for land with rich soil and planted vineyards, where they grew grapes to make wine. Despite many hardships, farmers learned how to survive on the western fields. A good harvest was always a reason to celebrate!

(below) These Dukhobor women worked hard in the fields. On western farms, everyone in the family had plenty of work to do!

BUSY NEW TOWNS

Not all the western settlers became farmers. Many people lived in towns. Miners, storeowners, and surveyors are just a few examples of townspeople. **Boomtowns** were fast-growing towns whose population seemed to explode overnight. Many boomtowns grew as a result of the gold rushes and the building of the railroad. Cities such as San Francisco and Dawson City started as boomtowns.

(left) A Chinese parade, complete with a ceremonial dragon, marches through an early western boomtown.

Rail and mining towns

Many of the original towns in the West were along the railway line. The railway brought thousands of settlers west. It also connected mining towns and farming communities to markets in the East. Crops that were grown in the West and minerals that were mined there were shipped to the cities in the East, where they were sold. Tools and other supplies from eastern cities came by rail to the West. As more and more businesses became involved in selling goods, new towns formed all over the West.

Here today, gone tomorrow

Western towns were built quickly and many of the buildings were unstable. Natural disasters such as tornadoes and fires could ruin a town in a day. A drought could slowly cripple a town until people simply gave up and left. Sometimes so many people arrived at once that unemployment was a problem. Nearly all western towns were formed around a single industry, such as the railroad or a mine. If the railroad stopped coming to town or mining ended, the people left quickly as well.

The 24-hour town!

In the late 1800s, a Native territory known as "the District" was one of the most desirable places in which to live. A treaty ruled that the land was off-limits to white settlers. In 1889, however, President Benjamin Harrison made a deal—at noon on April 22, settlers would be allowed into the District. Few people lived in Guthrie, a small station in the District, but that was about to change. On the morning of the 22nd, thousands of people lined up on the District boundary line. At noon they took off! People raced towards Guthrie on trains, wagons, horses, bicycles, and even on foot! They quickly claimed land as their own and set up tents. By nightfall, Guthrie had received over 10,000 new citizens!

CHALLENGES AND SUCCESSES

The early West was called the Wild West—and for a very good reason! It was full of robbers, bandits, and gamblers. Many people did not want to bring their families to such a dangerous place. In addition to crime, the farmers who had settled on the plains found that life was challenging and lonely because neighbors were often many miles away.

As more families arrived, however, the West changed. Settlers elected officials to help run their towns and sheriffs to protect them. Towns continued to supply steady jobs for people who were willing to move west. Farmers learned how to produce better crops. In one century, the West changed from a wild place to one with established laws, farms, towns, and cities.

Myth and reality

The settlers had high hopes of finding great fortunes and an easier lifestyle. When they arrived in the West, however, they found that life was more challenging than they had expected. Settling the land took time, and not everyone prospered. Gradually railroads, farms, mines, and towns began to cover the landscape. Eventually, the West became states and provinces that extended the United States and Canada from sea to sea.

(opposite page) By the 1900s, western towns were more stable, and settlers were starting families and sending their children to school. (below) The West provided jobs and business opportunities for many people.

GLOSSARY

boomtown A town that grows quickly in population and wealth

claim An area of land owned by a person

colony A territory ruled by another country

crofter A farmer

Hudson's Bay Company A British fur-trading business located in the Hudson Bay region

immigrant A person who comes to live in a place far from where he or she was born

Louisiana Territory A large territory in central North America owned by France until the United States purchased it in 1803

mission A settlement built for the purpose of converting people to Christianity

mountain men Hunters and trappers who lived in unsettled western areas

prejudice A negative judgement about people based on their religion, race, or gender

prospector A person who searches for gold and other precious minerals

slave A person who is owned by another person and forced to work without pay

totem pole A tall wooden pole carved and painted with Native American symbols

trading post A place set up by a fur-trading company at which furs were traded for supplies

transcontinental line A railroad line that stretches from one end of the country to the other

vaquero A Mexican cowboy

wagon train A group of covered wagons in which many settlers traveled west

INDEX

ACKNOWLEDGMENTS

Illustrations and colorizations

Barbara Bedell: pages 16, 31

Bonna Rouse: pages 24 (both), 25

Photographs and reproductions

Confederation Life Gallery of Canadian History: page 9 (bottom)

Fotos International/Archive Photos: page 29

Glenbow Archives, Calgary: page 13 (bottom right)

Mark Horn: pages 11 (bottom), 14

Kansas State Historical Society: pages 15, 21 (top), 22 (top), 28 (top)

Clark James Mishler: page 9 (top)

Pecos National Historical Park, ©Roy Andersen: page 8

Pecos Pueblo, about 1500 ©1993 Tom Lovell, The Greenwich Workshop®, Inc. (detail): pages 6–7

Terry Redlin, *For Amber Waves of Grain*, The Hadley Companies, Bloomington, Minnesota: page 26

William Aiken Walker, *The Sunny South*, Robert M. Hicklin Jr., Inc., Spartanburg, South Carolina, Private Collection (detail): page 12

Samuel B. Waugh, *The Bay and Harbor of New York*, Museum of the City of New York (33.169.1), Gift of Mrs. R. Littlejohn: page 18 (top)

Western Canada Pictorial Index: pages 18 (bottom), 19 (top), 20 (both), 21 (middle), 22 (middle, bottom left and right), 27, 30

Wyoming Division of Cultural Resources: pages 13 (top and bottom left), 19 (bottom), 21 (bottom), 23 (all), 28 (bottom)

Other images by Digital Stock, Digital Vision, and Image Club Graphics